Income's Ingenious Optimization

Effective ways to minimize tax burdens and maximize earnings through proven legal planning strategies

Zoltan Hendrix

Contents

1 Chapter 1: Introduction to Tax Planning

Understanding your tax obligations is the first step towards effective tax planning. This involves familiarizing yourself with the relevant tax laws and regulations in your jurisdiction. These laws are constantly evolving, so staying updated is crucial. Resources like the IRS website (for US taxpayers) or your country's equivalent tax authority provide valuable information. Don't hesitate to consult with a qualified tax professional for personalized guidance, especially when dealing with complex situations or significant financial transactions. They can provide expert advice tailored to your specific circumstances, ensuring you remain compliant and optimize your tax position. Remember, understanding the basics is the foundation upon which you build a robust tax plan.

Setting clear financial goals is paramount. Before you begin any tax planning, define what you want to achieve financially, both in the short term and long term. Do you aim to purchase a home within the next five years? Are you saving for your children's education? Or perhaps focusing on early retirement? These goals will dictate your tax strategy. For example, if early retirement is a priority, maximizing contributions to tax-advantaged retirement accounts should be a core component of your plan. Conversely, if you're planning a major purchase, understanding the tax implications of that purchase can help you time it strategically. This proactive approach ensures your tax plan aligns with your overall financial aspirations.

Developing a personalized tax plan requires careful consideration of your individual financial circumstances. Your income, expenses, investments, and family situation all play a significant role. This plan shouldn't be a one-size-fits-all approach; it needs to be tailored to your unique needs. Consider factors such as your employment status (employee, self-employed, business owner), your investment portfolio, and any significant life events anticipated in the near future. A well-structured plan accounts for these individual factors and incorporates strategies to minimize your tax liability legally and ethically. Regular review and adjustments are essential, adapting the plan as your circumstances change.

Effective tax planning is not about finding loopholes; it's about strategically utilizing the tax laws to your advantage. This involves understanding deductions, credits, and other tax provisions available to you. For instance, claiming allowable business expenses, maximizing contributions to retirement accounts, or strategically timing capital gains can significantly reduce your overall tax burden. Remember to maintain accurate and organized financial records; this is crucial for supporting your tax filings and minimizing the risk of audits. Proper record-keeping allows for easy identification of deductible expenses and simplifies the tax preparation process.

Proactive tax planning is far more beneficial than reactive measures. Addressing your tax obligations proactively helps you avoid potential penalties and interest charges associated with late filings or incorrect calculations. It also allows you to make informed financial decisions throughout the year, optimizing your financial outcomes. This proactive approach empowers you to take control of your financial future, securing your financial well-being. It prevents stressful last-minute rushes and allows for more deliberate financial strategizing throughout the year, which leads to greater financial control and peace of mind. Remember, your financial health is a reflection of the soundness of your financial planning and management. This chapter only lays the groundwork; consistent effort and attention to detail are essential to ensure the long-term success of your tax planning endeavor.

1.1 Understanding Tax Laws

Navigating the complexities of tax laws can feel daunting, especially for beginners. However, understanding the fundamentals is crucial for effectively managing your finances and minimizing your tax burden. Remember, this isn't about finding loopholes; it's about legally optimizing your financial situation. Proactive planning allows for strategic decision-making, resulting in significant long-term savings. This understanding empowers you to make informed choices that benefit your overall financial health. Think of it as a puzzle—each piece representing a different aspect of the tax code, and the completed picture is a financially secure future.

The tax code itself is extensive, a complex network of rules, regulations, and exceptions. It changes frequently too, so staying updated is important. Don't be intimidated though. While complete mastery requires dedicated study, a basic understanding of core principles is achievable, and surprisingly straightforward once you grasp the fundamental concepts. This chapter will help you build a solid foundation for future learning. Start by focusing on the key elements relevant to your specific financial situation. Seek professional advice for situations that seem overly intricate; it's an investment that will frequently save you more than it costs.

Firstly, familiarize yourself with the different types of taxes. Federal income tax is usually the largest component for most individuals. State income taxes vary by location, some states having no income tax at all. Sales taxes affect purchases, while property taxes apply to real estate. Understanding the implications of each is vital for informed financial planning. Don't neglect to consider self-employment taxes either; these are particularly relevant if you're a freelancer or run your own business. They can represent a significant portion of your tax liability. It is prudent to learn about these taxes now to avoid painful surprises later.

Understanding your tax bracket is equally important. Your tax bracket determines the rate at which your income is taxed, impacting your overall liability. Higher income levels typically mean higher tax brackets. Effective planning involves strategies to keep your income within the most favorable bracket while still building wealth. Various legal strategies, which we'll explore in later chapters, will help you make the most of this. Don't confuse your tax bracket with your effective tax rate, the actual percentage of your income paid in taxes.

Beyond individual taxes, it's crucial to understand tax filing requirements and deadlines. These vary depending on your filing status (single, married filing jointly, etc.), and failing to meet deadlines can result in penalties. The Internal Revenue Service (IRS) provides comprehensive resources to assist in navigating these requirements, and utilizing them can save you considerable stress and potential financial penalties. Familiarize yourself with the IRS website and the various tools available, like their interactive tax assistant.

Beyond the technical aspects, consider the broader context. Taxes fund essential public services like education, infrastructure, and social security. Understanding how your tax dollars are used can increase your sense of civic engagement and enhance your overall understanding of the tax system, fostering a more positive perspective towards it. This understanding helps contextualize the system, providing a broader perspective beyond mere personal financial optimization.

Effective tax planning isn't a one-time event, but an ongoing process. Regularly review your financial situation and adjust your strategies as needed. Life changes, such as marriage, starting a family, or changing careers, significantly impact your tax obligations. Don't assume your current plan will always be optimal. Flexibility and adaptation are key to keeping your tax planning effective, and this means staying informed on new tax laws and regulations as they change. This ongoing process will prevent you from ever being behind the curve.

Lastly, remember that seeking professional help is not a sign of weakness but a sign of smart financial management. A tax advisor can provide personalized guidance based on your specific circumstances, ensuring that you are utilizing all available legal strategies to minimize your tax burden. They can also assist in navigating complex tax situations, saving you time and preventing costly mistakes. Their expertise ensures you aren't overlooking any opportunities for savings and reduces the risk of errors that can lead to audits and penalties. It is a wise investment in the long run.

1.2 Goal Setting & Planning

Effective tax planning isn't just about reacting to tax bills; it's about proactively shaping your financial future. This requires a clear vision of where you want to be financially and a well-defined plan to get there. Understanding your goals is the cornerstone of successful tax optimization.

Begin by defining your short-term and long-term financial aspirations. Are you saving for a down payment on a house? Planning for your children's education? Securing a comfortable retirement? Writing these goals down, however seemingly basic, provides clarity and direction. Quantify them whenever possible. Instead of "buy a house," aim for "save $50,000 for a down payment within three years." Specificity is crucial.

Next, create a timeline. Break down your long-term goals into manageable, short-term milestones. This allows for regular progress checks and adjustments to your strategy as needed. A three-year savings goal, for instance, could be broken into annual targets, ensuring consistent progress. Regular review is essential to maintain motivation and adapt to changing circumstances.

Consider your current financial situation. Evaluate your income, expenses, assets, and liabilities. This comprehensive assessment will highlight your current financial health and pinpoint areas for improvement. Analyze your spending habits to identify areas where you can potentially reduce expenses and redirect funds toward your savings goals. Understand the tax implications of all your financial decisions, a key aspect frequently overlooked.

Now, integrate tax considerations into your financial plan. Understand your tax bracket and how different financial decisions will impact your overall tax burden. For example, tax-advantaged investment accounts can significantly reduce your tax liability over time, helping you reach your goals faster. Proper planning takes into account the various legal tax benefits at your disposal, from deductions to credits, creating a long term strategic plan.

Consult a qualified tax professional. While this chapter provides valuable information, personal financial situations are complex. A professional can provide tailored advice based on your specific circumstances, ensuring your plan is both effective and legally sound. They can help navigate the intricacies of tax laws and suggest strategies tailored to your unique situation, and prevent costly mistakes.

Remember, this is an ongoing process. Your financial goals and circumstances will evolve over time. Regularly review and update your plan to reflect these changes. Flexibility is key to adapting to unforeseen events and maintaining a financially healthy path towards your goals. Your financial journey needs constant adjustments, staying flexible while sticking to the general plan.

Don't let the complexity of tax laws discourage you. With a well-defined plan and professional guidance, you can effectively minimize your tax burden while maximizing your earnings. Proactive tax planning is an investment in your financial future—an investment that will pay dividends for years to come. Take the time to establish strong financial foundations and build from there. Small consistent steps contribute to reaching significant long-term objectives. Don't underestimate the power of persistent progress. Strategic goal-setting and careful planning form the bedrock of successful tax optimization, laying the groundwork for future chapters of your financial strategy. With clear goals, a defined timeline, and professional advice, you are equipped to create a robust financial plan that supports your ambitions while minimizing your tax obligations, setting yourself on the path to secure and comfortable future. This proactive approach can potentially safeguard your financial well-being while offering considerable financial gains in the long run. Remember, your journey to financial security is a marathon, not a sprint. Consistent effort and well-informed decisions are essential for lasting success.

2 Chapter 2: Maximizing Deductions

Many individuals overlook the power of deductions to significantly reduce their tax burden. Understanding and strategically utilizing available deductions is crucial for optimizing your income. Don't let valuable tax savings slip through the cracks; this chapter will empower you to claim every eligible deduction.

Business expenses, often a significant source of deductions, require careful documentation. Keep meticulous records of all business-related expenditures, from office supplies to travel costs. Remember, receipts, invoices, and bank statements are your allies in substantiating your claims. Accurate record-keeping not only minimizes the risk of an audit but also ensures you claim the maximum permissible deductions. Consult a tax professional to confirm the deductibility of specific expenses unique to your business, avoiding costly mistakes and ensuring compliance with IRS regulations. Don't underestimate the importance of organizing your records; clear categorization simplifies the tax preparation process.

Working from home presents unique opportunities for claiming deductions. The home office deduction can be a substantial tax benefit for those who dedicate a portion of their home exclusively to business activities. However, eligibility hinges on strict guidelines, requiring the space to be your principal place of business, or used regularly and exclusively for business. The IRS carefully scrutinizes these claims, demanding precise calculations of eligible expenses, proportional to the space used for business. These calculations can encompass a portion of mortgage interest, rent, utilities, and insurance. Accurate record-keeping and clear separation of business and personal areas are critical for success. Seeking guidance from a tax professional ensures accurate calculations and minimizes the risk of rejection.

Charitable contributions offer another avenue for reducing your tax liability. Donations to qualified charities are often deductible, providing substantial tax savings depending on the amount and type of donation. This includes cash contributions, as well as property donations, if appropriately documented and valued. Remember, holding onto documentation such as receipts and appraisal documents is crucial for supporting the deduction. You can deduct up to 60% of your adjusted gross income (AGI) for cash contributions, though there are limitations on non-cash deductions. Understanding these limitations, and the specific requirements for each type of donation, is essential to maximizing your tax benefits from charitable giving. Don't hesitate to explore options such as donating appreciated assets; this strategy offers tax advantages beyond the simple charitable deduction.

Maximizing deductions is about more than just knowing what's deductible; it's about strategic planning. Proactively managing your finances throughout the year, consistently recording all eligible expenses, and actively seeking opportunities to increase deductions, puts you in control of your tax liability. This proactive approach, in contrast to a reactive one, transforms tax preparation from a daunting task into an opportunity to optimize your finances. Consider consulting with a financial advisor and tax professional; they can provide personalized guidance and suggest strategies that are tailored to your specific financial situation and future financial planning. This collaborative approach ensures that you take full advantage of every available deduction. Remember, diligent record-keeping, professional advice, and a well-defined strategy are the cornerstones of maximizing deductions and minimizing your tax burden. The result is not just tax savings, but improved financial health and security. A little forethought can yield significant long-term benefits, significantly impacting your overall financial well-being. This proactive approach to tax planning positions you for greater financial success.

2.1 Business Expense Deductions

Many business owners mistakenly believe only large expenses qualify for deductions. This is untrue. Even seemingly insignificant costs, when properly documented, can significantly reduce your tax burden. Meticulous record-keeping is paramount; think of it as building a strong financial foundation, brick by painstaking brick. Every receipt, invoice, and bank statement serves as evidence supporting your claims. Neglecting this crucial aspect can jeopardize your deductions, leading to unnecessary tax payments and potential audits. Remember, the IRS scrutinizes claims rigorously.

Accurate record-keeping isn't merely about accumulating documents; it's about organizing them efficiently. A well-organized system, be it digital or physical, allows for swift retrieval of necessary information when filing taxes. Consider using accounting software, categorized folders, or a combination of both. Regardless of your chosen method, ensure your records are easily accessible, clearly labeled, and readily auditable. This simple step transforms potentially chaotic paperwork into a powerful tool for tax optimization.

Beyond the basics of record-keeping, understanding which expenses are deductible is vital. The IRS provides comprehensive guidelines; however, navigating these can be challenging for beginners. Consulting a tax professional can offer invaluable support. They possess specialized knowledge, enabling them to pinpoint specific deductions you might overlook. This professional guidance ensures you claim every legitimate deduction, maximizing your tax savings. The cost of this consultation often pales in comparison to the potential tax savings realized.

Let's look at some common, often-overlooked, business expense deductions. Office supplies, for instance, are fully deductible. This includes pens, paper, printer ink, and even software subscriptions directly related to your business operations. Similarly, professional development courses and conferences directly improving your skills or knowledge relevant to your profession are deductible. This includes fees, travel expenses (flights, accommodations, etc.), and even meals if they are part of the conference program. Don't underestimate the power of these seemingly minor expenses – they accumulate!

Travel expenses constitute another significant category. If your business involves client meetings or industry events requiring travel, you can deduct expenses like airfare, train tickets, car rentals, and even mileage. Crucially, documentation is key: Keep detailed records of your trips, including itineraries and receipts for all expenses. Remember, only business-related travel is deductible; personal trips are not. The line between business and personal can sometimes blur, so maintaining clear and comprehensive documentation is crucial to avoid IRS scrutiny. Accurate record-keeping is your strongest defense.

Advertising and marketing costs are another significant, yet sometimes underutilized, area for deductions. This includes expenses related to website development, social media marketing, print advertising, and even promotional gifts. Each expense requires thorough documentation, connecting it directly to your business's marketing and advertising efforts. This area can represent considerable deductions, especially for businesses heavily reliant on marketing and sales. Maintain a clear, consistent record of your expenses. Remember: even seemingly minor expenditures, when aggregated, can add up to substantial tax savings.

Finally, remember the importance of staying updated on tax laws and regulations. These laws change, and understanding the current rules is crucial for maximizing deductions and avoiding potential penalties. The IRS website and reputable tax publications offer guidance, but consulting a tax professional provides personalized advice tailored to your specific situation. This proactive approach protects you from costly mistakes and ensures you stay compliant with the ever-evolving tax landscape. This is arguably the most important aspect of maximizing deductions and minimizing tax burdens. Proactive planning, thorough record-keeping, and expert consultation are the pillars of effective tax optimization.

2.2 Home Office Deductions

The home office deduction can be a significant benefit for those who work from home, even partially. It allows you to deduct a portion of your home-related expenses, directly reducing your taxable income. However, claiming this deduction requires careful adherence to IRS guidelines, making it crucial to understand the specific requirements and limitations. Failing to meet these criteria can result in an audit and potential penalties. This chapter will guide you through the process, ensuring you navigate it successfully.

Eligibility isn't simply about working from home; it hinges on the designated workspace being your principal place of business, or a place used exclusively and regularly for business. This means it must be your main workspace, not just a supplementary one. If you have a separate office, meeting this requirement is straightforward. However, if you use a corner of your bedroom or living room, you'll need to prove its dedicated use. Consistent and exclusive business use is key. Think of keeping detailed records—perhaps even photographs—as proof. Remember, the IRS scrutinizes these deductions closely.

Calculating the deduction can be done in two ways: the simplified method and the actual expense method. The simplified method is far easier. You deduct $5 per square foot of your home office, up to a maximum of 300 square feet. This maximum limits the deduction to $1500, simplifying your calculations. This method is particularly appealing for its simplicity, making it attractive to those wanting a straightforward approach. However, it may not be the most advantageous for everyone, especially those with larger home offices or significant business expenses.

Conversely, the actual expense method lets you deduct a portion of all qualifying home expenses, including mortgage interest, rent, utilities, insurance, and repairs. However, you only deduct the percentage of these expenses directly attributable to your home office. This requires calculating the ratio of your home office's square footage to the total square footage of your home. This percentage is then applied to each eligible expense. For instance, if your home office occupies 10% of your home's total space, you deduct 10% of your mortgage interest, utilities, and so forth. Accurate record-keeping is paramount here; meticulous documentation is your defense against potential audit challenges. This method offers the potential for a larger deduction, but it necessitates greater organizational effort and a deeper understanding of allowable expenses.

Choosing between the simplified and actual expense methods depends on your specific circumstances. If you're new to this and prefer simplicity, the simplified method is a clear winner. Its ease of use significantly reduces the time and effort involved in preparing your taxes. But, if you have significant home-related expenses and a larger home office, the actual expense method might result in a more substantial deduction, despite the increased complexity. Analyze both; the best approach will depend on your specific financial situation.

Beyond the direct calculation of the deduction, remember the importance of comprehensive record-keeping. Maintaining detailed records is not merely advisable; it's essential. The IRS expects proof to support your deduction claims. These records should include receipts for all relevant expenses, detailed calculations of the square footage ratio, and clear documentation of your home office's exclusive use. This includes the photos mentioned earlier and a clear description of how you use your home office space. These aren't mere suggestions; they are vital safeguards to protect you from potential disputes. Don't underestimate the importance of a well-organized filing system, designed to withstand rigorous scrutiny.

Finally, remember that consulting with a tax professional can provide invaluable support. While this chapter offers guidance, individual situations can be complex. A qualified professional can analyze your unique circumstances, helping you determine the most advantageous method, ensuring compliance, and maximizing your potential deduction. Their expertise can help navigate the intricacies of tax laws, preventing errors and potentially significant financial repercussions. Consider this an investment in your financial well-being, providing peace of mind and possibly substantial tax savings. Seeking expert advice, especially when dealing with potentially complicated financial decisions, is a proactive measure that minimizes risk and maximizes benefits.

2.3 Charitable Contributions

Donating to charity offers significant tax advantages, reducing your overall tax burden while supporting worthy causes. Understanding the intricacies of these deductions is crucial for maximizing their benefit. Remember, the IRS requires meticulous record-keeping; without proper documentation, your deductions may be disallowed. Always retain receipts, bank statements, and any correspondence confirming your donations.

The types of contributions eligible for deduction vary. Cash donations, whether made directly or through payroll deduction programs, are straightforward to claim. However, non-cash contributions, such as donating used clothing or household goods, require careful consideration. These items must be in good condition, and you'll need a detailed list of the items donated and their fair market value at the time of the donation. For larger non-cash gifts, obtaining a written appraisal from a qualified expert might be necessary.

Appraisals can be costly, so weigh the potential tax savings against the appraisal fee. The value you claim can't exceed the item's fair market value—an overestimation can lead to penalties. Be prepared to justify your valuation to the IRS if audited. This meticulous record-keeping is paramount; even minor discrepancies can raise red flags. Organize your donation records systematically, preferably in a dedicated file or using accounting software designed for tax purposes.

Remember, the amount you can deduct is limited, often capped at a certain percentage of your adjusted gross income (AGI). This percentage varies based on the type of charity and the nature of your contribution. For instance, donations to public charities typically have a more generous deduction limit compared to those made to private foundations. Consulting a tax professional can help you navigate these complexities and ensure you are maximizing your deductions within legal limits.

Beyond the immediate tax benefits, strategic charitable giving can help you achieve long-term financial goals. For example, creating a donor-advised fund (DAF) allows you to make larger donations in a tax-advantaged manner over several years. This approach can be beneficial for high-income earners who are nearing a high tax bracket or are planning to pay substantial capital gains taxes in a particular year. A DAF provides flexibility, letting you make charitable contributions when it aligns strategically with your financial planning, even if it doesn't happen at the moment of the donation. It is a useful tool for financial planning, enabling well-structured charitable gifting.

Furthermore, carefully consider the long-term implications of your contributions. Donating appreciated assets, such as stocks held for over one year, offers additional tax benefits. You can deduct the fair market value of the assets at the time of donation while avoiding capital gains taxes, significantly impacting your overall tax liability. It is important to plan for this kind of strategy, always keeping in mind that the specifics will change as tax codes are periodically updated. Thus, keeping informed about the latest regulations is vital.

While charitable contributions offer compelling financial incentives, it's crucial to remember the ethical implications. Choose organizations whose missions resonate with your values and that demonstrate transparency and accountability in their operations. Verify their legitimacy through reputable sources before making significant donations. Your charitable giving should align with your personal values and the purpose of the cause supported; this way, you'll support the worthy causes that resonate with you and minimize your tax burden. The satisfaction of supporting a meaningful cause can amplify the benefits of charitable giving.

Don't solely focus on the tax advantages; let altruism guide your decision-making. Your contribution should be guided by your commitment to your selected cause. By carefully planning your charitable giving and maintaining accurate records, you can simultaneously support deserving causes and optimize your financial strategies for long-term success. This dual approach will create a positive impact that extends beyond the tax benefits, ultimately rewarding you both financially and emotionally. The blend of financial prudence and charitable giving offers a powerful combination, maximizing your impact in multiple facets of your life. Always remember that the tax benefits are a secondary bonus, with the impact on your community and your personal values being the real reward.

3 Chapter 3: Investment Strategies

Diversification isn't just a buzzword; it's the cornerstone of smart investing. Think of your investment portfolio as a carefully constructed bridge, each asset representing a supporting beam. A single, heavily weighted beam might buckle under pressure, but a diverse array of strong, independent beams distributes the load effectively, increasing the bridge's resilience. Similarly, spreading your investments across different asset classes—stocks, bonds, real estate—reduces your overall risk. A downturn in one sector won't cripple your entire portfolio. This strategic approach necessitates understanding your risk tolerance. Are you comfortable with the potential for higher returns, accepting greater volatility in exchange? Or do you prioritize stability and capital preservation, opting for lower-risk investments with potentially lower rewards? Honestly assessing your risk appetite is paramount to choosing the right investment mix for your financial goals.

Tax-advantaged accounts, such as 401(k)s and IRAs, offer significant benefits for long-term wealth accumulation. They provide tax deductions for contributions, reducing your immediate tax burden. This means more money in your pocket now, and more money growing tax-deferred in the account. Moreover, the growth of your investment within these accounts isn't taxed until you withdraw in retirement. It's like having a personal tax shelter for your investments. However, understanding the rules and regulations is crucial. Contribution limits vary, and there are specific withdrawal guidelines to avoid penalties. Take the time to learn about the different types of IRAs (Traditional vs. Roth) and understand which one aligns best with your individual financial situation and long-term retirement planning strategy. Careful planning can significantly benefit your long-term wealth accumulation.

Real estate, a tangible asset, presents unique opportunities for wealth building and tax advantages. Owning property offers potential rental income, generating a consistent cash flow. Furthermore, depreciation allows you to deduct a portion of your property's value each year, reducing your taxable income. However, real estate investment also comes with significant responsibilities. Property management, maintenance, and potential vacancy periods are factors to consider. Thorough due diligence is critical, including researching the property's location, assessing rental market demands, and reviewing financial statements. Consult with a real estate professional and a tax advisor to fully understand the financial and tax implications before making a purchase. Don't rush into it; proper research and understanding of the implications will increase your chances of success.

The stock market, often perceived as volatile, is capable of substantial growth over the long term. However, it's also susceptible to short-term fluctuations. A well-defined strategy is crucial. Investing in index funds or ETFs offers diversification across a broad range of companies, reducing individual stock risk. Dollar-cost averaging—investing a fixed amount at regular intervals—mitigates the impact of market volatility. Regardless of your approach, remember that the stock market requires patience and a long-term perspective. Short-term gains and losses should not distract from your overall investment strategy. Consider your long-term financial goals and risk tolerance when deciding what type of investment strategy is best for you.

Bonds, representing loans to corporations or governments, offer a different investment profile than stocks. They generally provide lower returns but are typically less volatile. Bonds can offer a degree of stability in your portfolio, counterbalancing the risk associated with stocks. The interest earned on many bonds is taxable, but some municipal bonds are exempt from federal income tax, which is a crucial factor for tax-efficient investment planning. Understanding different bond types (corporate bonds, municipal bonds, Treasury bonds) and their maturity dates will help you make informed decisions that fit your financial goals. Diversifying across various bond types can also reduce your portfolio's overall risk. Remember that even with lower risk, it's still important to consider diversification and to manage your expectations for returns.

Investing wisely involves more than simply choosing the right assets; it's about integrating your investment strategy with your overall tax planning. Understanding how different investments affect your tax liability is paramount. Tax-efficient strategies can significantly enhance your returns. It is essential to regularly review your portfolio and adjust your approach based on changes in your financial situation, market conditions, or your overall tax strategy. Tax laws and regulations change, so staying informed is crucial for the long-term success of your investment plan. Don't hesitate to seek advice from qualified professionals such as financial advisors and tax experts. Their guidance can be invaluable in navigating the complex world of finance.

3.1 Diversification & Risk

Diversification isn't just a buzzword; it's the bedrock of sound investment strategy. Think of your investment portfolio as a sturdy three-legged stool: stocks, bonds, and real estate. Each leg represents a different asset class, each with its own risk profile and return potential. A well-balanced portfolio, like a well-constructed stool, offers stability and resilience against market fluctuations. Ignoring diversification is like removing a leg—your entire financial structure becomes dangerously unstable.

Building a diversified portfolio requires careful consideration of your risk tolerance and financial goals. Are you a conservative investor prioritizing capital preservation, or are you more aggressive, seeking higher returns with a corresponding increase in risk? Your age also plays a critical role. Younger investors generally have a longer time horizon to recover from market downturns, allowing them to tolerate more risk. Older investors, nearing retirement, often prioritize stability and income generation. Understanding your personal risk profile is paramount before making any investment decisions. It guides you towards choosing a portfolio mix aligned with your comfort level and financial objectives. Don't just blindly follow trends; personalize your strategy for optimal results.

Stocks, traditionally considered riskier, offer the potential for high returns over the long term. However, they are subject to significant price fluctuations, making them less suitable for risk-averse investors, especially those approaching retirement. Bonds, on the other hand, are generally considered less volatile, offering more stability. Government bonds, in particular, are often viewed as relatively low-risk investments because of their backing by the government. However, their returns might be comparatively lower. Real estate investments provide a different dimension, offering potential appreciation and rental income but also demanding higher initial capital outlay, carrying costs, and the risk of property value decline. Finding the right balance between these asset classes is crucial for effective diversification.

Tax-advantaged accounts, like 401(k)s and IRAs, are powerful tools in your diversification arsenal. These accounts not only allow you to grow your investments tax-deferred or tax-free, but they also offer significant diversification opportunities within their structures. You can invest in a wide range of assets within these accounts, aligning your holdings with your broader investment strategy, risk tolerance and retirement goals. Failing to maximize contributions to these accounts means forfeiting valuable tax benefits and limiting your potential for long-term growth, hence the crucial role it plays in the diversification strategy. Knowing the intricacies and nuances of the different types of accounts, contribution limits, and associated tax laws is essential to effectively leverage them.

Beyond the traditional asset classes, consider alternative investments like commodities or precious metals. These can provide a hedge against inflation or economic uncertainty, adding another layer of diversification to your portfolio. However, these alternative assets often come with higher risks and require more specialized knowledge. It is vital to thoroughly research these alternative options before allocating any significant portion of your portfolio to them.

Remember, diversification isn't a one-time event; it's an ongoing process. Regularly review your portfolio, rebalancing your assets as needed to maintain your target asset allocation. Market conditions change, your financial goals evolve, and your risk tolerance might shift over time. A dynamic approach ensures your portfolio remains aligned with your circumstances and your objectives. This regular rebalancing is not just about maintaining percentages but is about ensuring your financial structure is resilient.

While diversification significantly reduces risk, it doesn't eliminate it entirely. No investment is entirely risk-free. Thorough due diligence is vital before investing in any asset. Understand the potential risks involved, research the companies or funds you're considering, and seek professional advice when needed. Diversification provides a safety net; however, it does not guarantee that you will make money. It's just a strategy to minimize your losses.

Finally, don't underestimate the power of professional guidance. A financial advisor can provide personalized advice based on your individual circumstances, helping you craft a diversified portfolio tailored to your risk tolerance and financial goals. They can help you navigate complex tax laws, maximizing tax advantages and optimizing your investment strategy. A well-structured financial plan, guided by a professional, offers a clearer path towards financial security. The support and guidance of an expert is invaluable in handling the complexity of tax laws and optimizing investments. Remember, seeking professional advice is an investment in your financial future.

3.2 Tax-Advantaged Accounts

Tax-advantaged accounts offer a powerful tool for wealth building while simultaneously reducing your tax burden. Understanding how these accounts function is crucial for long-term financial success. They essentially allow you to shelter a portion of your income from immediate taxation, leading to significant savings over time. This strategy isn't just for high-income earners; even modest savings can benefit substantially.

Several types of tax-advantaged accounts exist, each with its own set of rules and benefits. Retirement accounts, such as 401(k)s and traditional IRAs, are perhaps the most well-known. Contributions to these plans are often tax-deductible, meaning the money you put in isn't taxed immediately. However, remember, you'll pay taxes when you withdraw the funds in retirement. This delay in taxation allows your investments to grow tax-free, compounding your returns over the years. This deferral of tax liability is a significant advantage. The specific contribution limits and rules vary, so careful research is vital to maximize your contribution and avoid penalties.

Beyond retirement, other tax-advantaged options exist. Health savings accounts (HSAs) are designed to pay for eligible medical expenses. Contributions are tax-deductible, the funds grow tax-free, and withdrawals for qualified medical expenses are also tax-free – a triple tax advantage! These accounts can be particularly beneficial for those enrolled in high-deductible health plans. It's a smart approach to planning for future healthcare costs.

Another lesser-known option is the 529 plan, designed for education savings. These plans offer tax benefits on both contributions and growth, making them a powerful tool for families saving for college or other qualified education expenses. While contributions aren't tax deductible at the federal level (state laws vary), the earnings grow tax-free, and withdrawals for qualified education expenses are also tax-free. Planning for your child's education well in advance can greatly reduce the financial strain. Understand your state's tax benefits, as incentives differ.

The key to maximizing the effectiveness of tax-advantaged accounts lies in strategic planning and understanding the specific rules governing each account type. For instance, premature withdrawals from retirement accounts may result in significant penalties, substantially reducing their overall tax advantage. Similarly, using HSA funds for non-medical expenses can lead to tax implications. Carefully reviewing the rules and regulations for each account type is essential before making contributions or withdrawals. Always consult with a qualified financial advisor to develop a personalized plan that aligns with your specific financial situation and goals.

Your understanding of your own financial landscape and risk tolerance dictates the best combination of accounts for you. Do you prefer the certainty of a Roth IRA, where contributions aren't tax-deductible, but withdrawals are tax-free in retirement? Or, does the tax deductibility of a traditional IRA appeal more to you, despite the fact that withdrawals will be taxed? These questions must be addressed and carefully considered.

Moreover, contributing to tax-advantaged accounts is not merely about minimizing your tax bill; it's about fostering a disciplined savings habit. The automatic deduction from your paycheck into a 401(k) can be a very powerful tool for saving, as you never actually "see" that money. The tax benefits act as an incentive, encouraging you to save more for your future. The discipline of consistent savings, coupled with the tax benefits of these accounts, is a recipe for long-term financial prosperity. It's vital to understand how these plans work within the context of your larger financial strategy.

It's prudent to diversify your investments within your tax-advantaged accounts. Don't put all your eggs in one basket, so to speak. Consider a mix of stocks, bonds, and other suitable assets, always considering your risk tolerance and investment goals. Diversification minimizes potential losses and maximizes returns over time. While tax benefits are essential, remember that financial success hinges on a broad, well-structured investment portfolio. A qualified financial advisor can help you with this.

Finally, remember to regularly review your tax-advantaged accounts. Ensure your beneficiary designations are up to date, and check that your investment strategy still aligns with your financial objectives. Your financial situation and goals will change over time. Annual reviews are crucial to ensure these accounts continue to serve their intended purpose effectively. Proactive management is essential to maintain and maximize the full benefit of these valuable financial tools.

3.3 Real Estate Investing

Real estate offers a powerful avenue for wealth creation and tax optimization, but requires careful planning. Understanding the tax implications of various real estate ventures is crucial for maximizing returns and minimizing your tax burden. Don't jump in blindly; thorough research and professional advice are invaluable.

Unlike other investments, real estate provides tangible assets with potential for appreciation and passive income streams. Rental properties, for instance, generate cash flow which can offset expenses and potentially lower your taxable income. However, the complexities of depreciation, capital gains, and property taxes require a systematic approach.

Depreciation is a significant tax advantage available to property owners. It allows you to deduct a portion of your property's cost over its useful life, reducing your taxable income each year. The calculation depends on factors like the property type, its intended use, and the chosen depreciation method—straight-line or accelerated—each with different implications. Understanding these nuances is key to properly utilizing depreciation.

Beyond depreciation, there are various other tax deductions you can claim related to your real estate investment. These include mortgage interest payments, property taxes, repairs and maintenance costs, and insurance premiums. Accurately tracking these expenses is paramount; meticulous record-keeping prevents potential auditing issues and ensures you claim every deduction you're entitled to. Consult a tax professional for guidance on specific deductions applicable to your situation.

Investing in real estate also opens doors to certain tax credits, depending on your location and specific circumstances. These credits can significantly reduce your overall tax liability. For example, some localities offer credits for rehabilitating historic buildings or for building energy-efficient properties. Research available credits within your area, as these can be substantial. Keep abreast of legislative changes to ensure you don't miss out on new opportunities.

Tax-deferred exchanges, also known as 1031 exchanges, provide a powerful strategy for minimizing capital gains taxes when selling investment properties. This mechanism allows you to defer paying capital gains taxes by reinvesting the proceeds into a like-kind property within a specific timeframe. While seemingly complex, 1031 exchanges can dramatically increase your long-term wealth by avoiding immediate tax burdens. The rules are intricate though, so expert guidance is highly recommended.

However, real estate investing is not without its risks. Fluctuations in the market, unexpected maintenance costs, and tenant issues can significantly impact your profitability. Thorough due diligence is paramount. Research property values, analyze rental market trends, and carefully assess the potential risks before investing. A thorough understanding of the local market and the condition of a specific property is essential to make an informed decision.

Furthermore, financing your real estate investments carefully is critical. While leveraging debt can amplify returns, excessive borrowing can lead to financial strain if rental income falls short. Always consider your debt-to-income ratio and carefully assess your ability to meet your mortgage payments even during periods of low occupancy. Secure financing that aligns with your risk tolerance and financial goals. Consider seeking advice from a financial advisor experienced in real estate financing to create a strong strategy.

Finally, don't underestimate the value of professional advice. Working with a real estate agent experienced in investments, a tax advisor specializing in real estate, and a financial planner can make all the difference in creating a successful and tax-efficient investment strategy. Their expertise will guide you through the complexities of the market, help you avoid costly mistakes, and ultimately maximize your long-term profitability. The initial investment in professional guidance is a crucial step towards building a strong and lasting foundation for your real estate portfolio.

3.4 Stock Market Strategies

Successful stock market investing requires a blend of understanding, patience, and strategic planning. It's not about get-rich-quick schemes; it's about building long-term wealth while minimizing your tax burden, a crucial aspect covered extensively in previous chapters. Remember, consistent, informed choices yield far better results than impulsive, high-risk bets. This chapter will provide you with actionable steps, focussing on methods that align with the tax optimization strategies outlined earlier in the book.

Begin by defining your investment goals. What are you hoping to achieve? Are you saving for retirement, a down payment on a house, or something else entirely? Your goals will dictate your investment timeline and risk tolerance. A long-term goal, such as retirement, allows for more aggressive investing; conversely, short-term goals might necessitate a more conservative approach. Clarifying this will help you create a tailored strategy that aligns perfectly with your overall financial plan, and remember this directly impacts your tax planning, aligning with the foundation we laid in the introductory chapter.

Diversification is paramount. Don't put all your eggs in one basket. Spread your investments across different asset classes, such as stocks, bonds, and potentially real estate, as discussed in a previous chapter. This reduces your overall risk. Consider different sectors as well; a portfolio heavily weighted in one sector is vulnerable to industry-specific downturns. Diversification minimizes this exposure. Remember, a diverse portfolio also helps in optimizing tax benefits because different assets are subject to different tax treatments.

Understand the different types of stock investments. Common stock gives you ownership in a company and the right to vote on corporate matters. Preferred stock offers a dividend but usually doesn't provide voting rights. Each has its own tax implications, which could affect your overall tax strategy. Therefore, studying the differences and choosing appropriately is crucial to maximizing your returns whilst minimizing your tax liabilities.

Research and select stocks carefully. Don't blindly follow tips or market hype. Thoroughly research companies before investing, analyzing their financial statements, business model, and competitive landscape. Look for companies with a strong track record of profitability and sustainable growth. Consider also the long-term projections, as this significantly impacts your long-term returns, and subsequently, your tax implications. Remember, due diligence is essential to limit risk and make informed investment decisions.

Consider dollar-cost averaging. Instead of investing a lump sum at once, invest smaller amounts regularly over time. This strategy helps mitigate the risk of market volatility. If the market falls, you'll buy more shares at lower prices. If it rises, you'll still be consistently adding to your investment. This systematic approach reduces the impact of short-term market fluctuations, allowing for a more consistent and steady growth. It also offers better tax planning flexibility by spreading out the tax liability over time.

Be patient and disciplined. The stock market fluctuates. Don't panic sell during market downturns. Instead, stick to your investment plan and remain disciplined in your approach. Avoid emotional decision-making; this is a common trap for new investors, and this disciplined approach will help ensure better long-term financial success, which in turn benefits your overall tax optimization.

Regularly review and rebalance your portfolio. Market conditions change, and so should your investment strategy. Periodically review your portfolio's performance and rebalance it to maintain your desired asset allocation. This will ensure that your investments continue to align with your goals, risk tolerance, and tax optimization strategy. Continual monitoring helps to mitigate potential risks.

Stay informed about tax laws and regulations. Tax laws change, and understanding these changes is critical for maximizing your returns and minimizing your tax liability. Stay updated on relevant tax laws to ensure that your investment strategies remain compliant and effective in minimizing your tax burdens. This ties in directly with the themes covered in the initial chapters of this book.

Remember, investing in the stock market involves risk. There's no guarantee of profit. However, by following these strategies and utilizing the tax optimization techniques outlined in this book, you'll significantly improve your chances of success and minimize the tax burden on your hard-earned gains. This approach marries sound investment practices with effective tax planning, ensuring a synergistic approach to wealth building. It's about building a sustainable long-term strategy.

3.5 Bond Investments

Bond investments offer a relatively stable and predictable income stream, a crucial aspect of any sound financial strategy, especially for those seeking to minimize tax burdens while maximizing earnings. Unlike stocks, which are subject to market volatility, bonds represent a loan you make to a government or corporation, earning interest payments in return. This predictable income can be a cornerstone of your long-term financial plan, providing a reliable buffer against market fluctuations. Understanding the different types of bonds is paramount to making informed investment choices.

Treasury bonds, issued by the U.S. government, are considered among the safest investments available, backed by the full faith and credit of the government. Municipal bonds, issued by state and local governments, often offer tax advantages, particularly for investors residing within the issuing municipality. Corporate bonds, issued by companies, carry more risk than government bonds but typically offer higher yields to compensate for that increased risk. The risk-reward trade-off must be carefully weighed against your individual tolerance and financial goals.

Diversification within your bond portfolio is key to mitigating risk. Don't put all your eggs in one basket, so to speak. Spreading your investments across various issuers, maturities, and bond types reduces the impact of any single bond defaulting or experiencing a significant decline in value. This diversification strategy is not merely a matter of spreading out the risk; it's a fundamental principle for reducing volatility and ensuring greater stability in your portfolio's performance. Consider a blend of government, municipal, and corporate bonds, tailoring the mix to align with your risk tolerance and financial objectives.

The tax implications of bond investments can be significant. Interest earned on most bonds is taxable at the federal level, while the state and local tax implications vary depending on the type of bond and your residency. Municipal bonds, as previously noted, often offer tax-exempt interest, making them particularly attractive for high-income taxpayers in higher tax brackets. Understanding these tax implications and strategically incorporating tax-advantaged bonds into your portfolio can significantly impact your overall tax liability and consequently your net returns.

Before investing in any bond, thorough due diligence is critical. Examine the issuer's creditworthiness, analyzing their financial statements and credit ratings to assess their ability to repay the principal and make timely interest payments. Consider the bond's maturity date, which determines when you'll receive your principal back, and understand the impact of interest rate fluctuations on bond prices. Remember, bond prices generally move inversely to interest rates; rising rates can decrease bond prices and vice versa. This inverse relationship is a critical factor in bond valuation and must be considered when constructing your portfolio. Professional guidance from a financial advisor can prove invaluable, especially if navigating the complexities of bond investing feels overwhelming.

Timing your bond purchases can influence your returns. If interest rates are expected to rise, it's generally prudent to invest in short-term bonds, to avoid locking in a lower yield for a longer period. Conversely, if rates are anticipated to fall, longer-term bonds could be a more attractive option. This requires careful consideration of prevailing economic conditions and interest rate forecasts. It's important to note that predicting interest rate movements with certainty is virtually impossible. While forecasts can be helpful, they don't eliminate risk.

The yield curve, a graphical representation of interest rates across different maturities, can be an informative tool in making investment decisions. A steep yield curve generally suggests expectations of future interest rate increases, while a flat or inverted curve indicates the opposite. This insight can inform decisions on the maturity of bonds to purchase, optimizing returns based on your expectations of market movements. Understanding this concept contributes significantly to intelligent investment strategies.

Bond funds offer a diversified approach to bond investing, allowing you to participate in a range of bonds with a single investment. These funds are managed by professionals who actively select and manage a portfolio of bonds, often reducing the workload and the requirement for extensive individual research. However, remember that bond funds have their own fees and expenses, so it's crucial to evaluate the fund's expense ratio before investing to ensure that the fees are reasonable and not unduly impacting your returns.

Finally, remember that bond investments are not without risk. Default risk, the possibility of the issuer failing to repay the principal and interest, is always present. Interest rate risk, as mentioned earlier, can impact the value of your bonds. Inflation risk, the erosion of purchasing power due to rising prices, can diminish the real return on your investments. While bonds offer more stability than stocks, they are not risk-free. A well-diversified portfolio and a thorough understanding of these potential risks is essential for successful bond investing. Continuously monitoring your portfolio and adjusting your strategy as needed will be vital to protecting and growing your wealth responsibly.

4 Chapter 4: Retirement Planning

Securing your financial future requires careful planning, particularly concerning retirement. While previous chapters focused on immediate tax optimization, this chapter shifts the perspective to long-term financial well-being. Understanding the tax implications of retirement savings is crucial to maximizing your nest egg.

Retirement planning isn't simply about saving money; it's about strategically structuring your savings to minimize your tax burden both now and in retirement. Failing to plan properly can severely impact your retirement income, leaving you with less than you anticipated. Therefore, a proactive approach is essential.

The most common vehicles for retirement savings are 401(k)s and IRAs. 401(k)s, offered through employers, often include employer matching contributions, essentially free money. These contributions are typically pre-tax, reducing your current taxable income. However, withdrawals in retirement are taxed as ordinary income. IRAs, on the other hand, offer greater flexibility but come with different contribution limits and tax implications. Traditional IRAs offer similar pre-tax benefits to 401(k)s, while Roth IRAs, while not offering immediate tax benefits, provide tax-free withdrawals in retirement.

Choosing between a traditional and Roth IRA depends entirely on your individual circumstances and predictions about your future tax bracket. If you anticipate being in a higher tax bracket in retirement, a Roth IRA could be more advantageous. Conversely, if you believe your tax bracket will be lower in retirement, a traditional IRA might be preferable. Careful consideration of your current income, projected retirement income, and anticipated tax rates is necessary to make an informed decision. Consulting a financial advisor can prove invaluable in navigating these complexities.

Beyond 401(k)s and IRAs, pensions and annuities offer additional retirement income streams. Pensions, once common, are becoming less prevalent, but if you have access to one, it represents a guaranteed stream of income. The tax implications vary depending on the pension plan's structure. Annuities, on the other hand, offer more flexibility, but also come with fees and complexities. They can provide a steady stream of income throughout retirement, but understanding the various types—immediate or deferred, fixed or variable—is essential to make a well-informed choice that aligns with your risk tolerance and financial goals.

Consider diversifying your retirement portfolio across different asset classes, reducing your overall risk. While bonds offer stability, stocks generally offer higher growth potential, but also increased volatility. A balanced portfolio reflects your risk tolerance and long-term financial objectives. Regularly rebalancing your portfolio to maintain this balance is critical, ensuring you neither overexpose nor underexpose yourself to any single asset class.

Your retirement strategy shouldn't be static; it should adapt to your changing circumstances. Regularly review your investment strategy, adjusting your asset allocation as your needs and financial situation evolve. Unexpected events—illness, job loss, or market downturns—may require adjustments to your plan, potentially delaying your retirement or necessitating changes to your withdrawal strategy. Therefore, periodic review, perhaps annually, ensures your plan remains suitable.

Effective retirement planning is a long-term commitment, requiring consistent contributions and strategic investment choices. Don't underestimate the power of compound interest; starting early, even with small contributions, allows your investments to grow significantly over time. Remember, your retirement income is directly linked to your investment growth and carefully planned tax-efficient savings. The earlier you start, the more you benefit from the magic of compounding.

Don't hesitate to seek professional advice. Financial advisors can help you create a personalized retirement plan tailored to your specific needs, taking into account your age, risk tolerance, and financial goals. They can also guide you through the complex tax implications of various retirement savings plans and investment strategies, ensuring your plan aligns with both your short-term and long-term financial objectives. Remember, a well-structured plan significantly increases your chances of enjoying a comfortable and secure retirement. Procrastination is your worst enemy when it comes to planning for your financial future. Start now; your future self will thank you.

4.1 401(k) & IRA Plans

401(k)s and Individual Retirement Accounts (IRAs) are cornerstones of a robust retirement plan, offering significant tax advantages. Understanding their nuances is crucial for maximizing your savings and minimizing your tax burden. A 401(k) is a retirement savings plan sponsored by your employer, allowing pre-tax contributions to be deducted from your paycheck, effectively lowering your taxable income in the present. This reduction translates to immediate tax savings. Contributions typically grow tax-deferred, meaning you only pay taxes upon withdrawal in retirement. Many employers offer matching contributions, a valuable incentive that essentially boosts your savings. You should understand the specifics of your employer's plan, including contribution limits and vesting schedules, to take full advantage.

The tax advantages associated with 401(k) plans are considerable, making them an attractive option for most individuals. Pre-tax contributions significantly reduce current taxable income, providing immediate savings. Furthermore, investment earnings grow tax-deferred, meaning you only pay taxes when you withdraw the money in retirement, often at a lower tax bracket. The potential for employer matching contributions further enhances the attractiveness of 401(k) plans, effectively doubling (or even tripling) your investment power.

IRAs, on the other hand, are individual retirement accounts that you set up yourself. The most common types are Traditional and Roth IRAs. Traditional IRAs offer tax-deductible contributions, lowering your current taxable income. Similar to 401(k) plans, the earnings grow tax-deferred, resulting in tax deferral until retirement. Roth IRAs, conversely, offer tax-free withdrawals in retirement. Contributions are not tax-deductible, but qualified withdrawals and earnings are tax-free, providing significant long-term tax advantages. The choice between a Traditional and Roth IRA depends on your current and projected future tax brackets. If you anticipate being in a higher tax bracket in retirement, a Roth IRA may be more beneficial.

Contribution limits for both 401(k)s and IRAs are subject to annual adjustments by the IRS. These limits should be carefully reviewed each year to optimize your contributions. While 401(k) plans generally have higher contribution limits than IRAs, the combined contribution limits from both accounts should be considered to maximize your tax-advantaged savings potential. Remember to also consider your overall financial situation, including other sources of retirement income and debts, when determining appropriate contribution levels. Don't overextend yourself financially, ensuring you maintain a comfortable cash flow to meet your immediate needs and handle emergencies.

Choosing between a 401(k) and an IRA, or utilizing both, depends on several factors. The availability of an employer-sponsored 401(k) is a primary consideration. If your employer offers a 401(k) with matching contributions, it often makes financial sense to maximize those contributions first, leveraging the free money provided by your employer. Following this strategy, you can then contribute to an IRA to the extent allowed by your income and contribution limits, diversifying your retirement savings across different accounts.

Regardless of which retirement plan(s) you choose, it's crucial to develop a comprehensive retirement savings strategy. Carefully consider your risk tolerance, investment timeline, and desired retirement lifestyle when selecting investments within these accounts. Regularly reviewing and rebalancing your portfolio as needed is essential to maintain a balanced approach and manage risk. Moreover, you should consult a qualified financial advisor who can help tailor a personalized retirement plan that aligns with your specific circumstances and financial goals. They can help you navigate the complexities of these plans and ensure you are making the most informed decisions. This expert guidance can be particularly valuable in addressing specialized circumstances.

In conclusion, understanding the differences between 401(k)s and IRAs is fundamental to effective retirement planning and tax optimization. Each plan offers unique tax advantages, and the optimal approach often involves a combination of both. By maximizing contributions within the established limits, you can significantly reduce your current tax liability and build a substantial retirement nest egg. Remember that proactive planning is key to ensuring a comfortable and secure financial future. Procrastination on this front can have significant financial consequences. Consider seeking professional advice to ensure your strategy aligns with your personal circumstances and aspirations.

4.2 Pension & Annuity Options

Pensions and annuities offer distinct pathways to retirement income, each with its own tax implications. Understanding these differences is crucial for optimizing your retirement plan and minimizing your tax burden. Pensions, often employer-sponsored, provide a regular, guaranteed income stream upon retirement. The amount received is typically based on factors like salary and years of service. Taxation of pension income varies; a portion might be tax-deferred during accumulation, while the distributions themselves are generally taxed as ordinary income in retirement. Careful planning is essential to account for this in your overall retirement strategy. It's wise to consult with a financial advisor to understand the specific tax implications of your particular pension plan.

Annuities, on the other hand, are contracts between you and an insurance company. You contribute money, either in a lump sum or over time, and the insurance company guarantees a future income stream, often for life. There are different types of annuities, each with varying levels of risk and tax treatment. Immediate annuities begin paying out immediately upon purchase, while deferred annuities offer a future income stream at a specified time. Fixed annuities provide a guaranteed rate of return, while variable annuities invest in market-linked accounts, providing potential for higher returns but also increased risk. The tax implications can be complex, varying depending on the type of annuity, how it's funded, and when you start receiving payments. Early withdrawals usually incur penalties, and the growth within the annuity might be tax-deferred until distribution. Understanding the tax implications of each type of annuity is vital for informed decision-making. Thorough research and professional financial advice are highly recommended before investing in any annuity.

A significant consideration is the interplay between pensions, annuities, and other sources of retirement income, such as Social Security. The overall income level significantly impacts your tax bracket, affecting your net retirement income. Careful coordination of your retirement income streams can help minimize your overall tax liability. For instance, strategically timing withdrawals from different accounts can help keep your income within a lower tax bracket, maximizing your after-tax income. This often involves meticulous planning and potentially adjusting your withdrawal schedule throughout your retirement years, accounting for changes in your tax situation. This strategic approach necessitates accurate projections of future income and expenses, including the potential impact of inflation and healthcare costs.

Many people underestimate the importance of professional guidance in navigating the complexities of pension and annuity taxation. A qualified financial advisor can analyze your specific circumstances, taking into account your existing investments, other income sources, and personal financial goals. They can help you model different retirement scenarios, evaluating the tax implications of various strategies. The personalized advice offered by a financial advisor can greatly enhance your ability to make informed and effective decisions regarding your retirement planning. The advisor can help you identify potential tax loopholes or advantages specific to your financial situation. They'll also keep you updated on any changes in tax laws or regulations that could affect your retirement income. This ongoing support can prove invaluable in maintaining a financially secure retirement while minimizing your tax obligations.

In conclusion, both pensions and annuities offer valuable pathways toward retirement security, but their tax implications differ significantly. Careful consideration of the tax consequences of each, in the context of your broader retirement strategy, is absolutely essential. Thorough research and the guidance of a qualified financial advisor are strongly recommended for optimizing your retirement income and minimizing your tax burden. Don't underestimate the long-term impact of even small tax savings. A well-planned strategy today can contribute significantly to a more comfortable and financially secure retirement tomorrow. Seeking professional advice ensures you are taking full advantage of available opportunities to maximize your retirement income while remaining compliant with tax regulations. Remember, proactive planning is key to a successful and stress-free retirement.

5 Chapter 5: Estate Planning Basics

Estate planning might seem daunting, but it's fundamentally about safeguarding your family's future. Think of it as a roadmap, guiding your assets to the right people after you're gone, minimizing potential tax burdens along the way. Proactive planning provides peace of mind, knowing your loved ones are protected.

A will is your primary tool for controlling the distribution of your assets. It dictates who inherits your property, from your house and car to your investments and personal belongings. Without a will, state laws determine the distribution, which may not align with your wishes, potentially leading to family disputes and unintended consequences. Consider seeking legal counsel to draft a will that accurately reflects your intentions, ensuring a smooth and conflict-free transition.

Trusts, on the other hand, offer more sophisticated asset management and protection. They allow you to appoint a trustee to manage your assets for the benefit of designated beneficiaries. This is particularly useful for protecting assets from creditors or managing inheritances for minors. Different types of trusts exist, each serving unique purposes. A revocable trust allows you to change or revoke the terms during your lifetime, while an irrevocable trust provides greater asset protection but limits your control. The choice depends heavily on your individual circumstances and goals.

Gift and estate taxes can significantly impact your legacy. Understanding the applicable thresholds and exemptions is crucial. Strategic gifting during your lifetime can reduce your taxable estate, benefiting both you and your heirs. Properly structured gifts, taking advantage of the annual gift tax exclusion, can minimize tax liabilities without sacrificing your financial well-being. This requires careful planning and ideally consultation with a tax advisor familiar with current regulations.

Beneficiary designations on accounts like retirement plans and life insurance policies are often overlooked but are critically important. These designations supersede your will, dictating who receives the proceeds upon your death. Ensuring these designations are up-to-date and align with your wishes prevents potential delays and complications in the distribution of these assets, simplifying the process for your loved ones during an already difficult time. Regularly reviewing and updating these designations is an essential aspect of effective estate planning, ensuring accuracy and alignment with your changing circumstances.

Consider consulting with a qualified estate planning attorney to create a comprehensive plan tailored to your specific needs. They can help you navigate the complexities of wills, trusts, and tax laws, ensuring your assets are distributed according to your wishes and that your family's financial future is secure. Don't underestimate the value of professional guidance; a well-structured estate plan offers more than just financial security; it provides peace of mind, knowing your affairs are handled responsibly and efficiently. Remember, this isn't just about money; it's about ensuring your legacy reflects your values and protects those you care about most. The process might seem complex initially, but the long-term benefits far outweigh the upfront effort.

Furthermore, your estate plan shouldn't be a static document. Life changes – marriage, divorce, the birth or death of family members, significant financial changes – all necessitate reviewing and updating your plan to reflect your current circumstances. Regular review, perhaps annually or after any significant life event, ensures your plan remains relevant and effectively protects your assets and your family's future. A regularly updated plan minimizes the risk of unforeseen complications and ensures your wishes are honored accurately. This proactive approach to estate planning safeguards your family's well-being long after you're gone. Ignoring this crucial aspect of financial planning could leave your loved ones vulnerable to unnecessary financial burdens and potential legal disputes. Remember, proactive planning offers not just financial security but also peace of mind, knowing you have done your best to secure a smooth transition for your family. Seek professional advice to customize your plan to reflect your unique family structure and financial circumstances. This personalized approach will be instrumental in optimizing your estate plan's efficiency.

The earlier you start planning, the better prepared you will be. Begin by gathering essential documents like birth certificates, marriage certificates, deeds, and financial statements. This inventory allows for a more accurate assessment of your assets and liabilities, forming the basis of your estate plan. It's essential to consider all possible scenarios and to have clear, documented plans in place to address them. This proactive approach will help streamline the process and minimize stress on your loved ones. By establishing a well-structured and comprehensive plan, you can confidently anticipate and manage unforeseen circumstances effectively and mitigate potential future challenges. Consider the impact of inflation and potential tax law changes when you are preparing long-term projections; it's not just about today's financial reality, but about securing your family's financial future.

5.1 Wills & Trusts

Wills and trusts are fundamental estate planning tools, offering significant tax advantages and control over asset distribution after your passing. A will, simply put, is a legal document outlining your wishes for the distribution of your assets. It dictates who inherits your property, designates guardians for minor children, and appoints an executor to manage your estate. Without a will, state laws determine asset distribution, potentially leading to unintended consequences and family disputes. This lack of control can be especially problematic in blended families or situations with complex asset holdings. Failing to plan can lead to lengthy and expensive probate processes, further delaying the distribution of your assets to your beneficiaries.

Understanding the different types of trusts is crucial for maximizing their tax benefits. Revocable living trusts allow you to maintain control over your assets during your lifetime, while offering the potential for probate avoidance after your death. These trusts are easily modified or revoked as your circumstances change, offering flexibility. Irrevocable trusts, on the other hand, provide more complex tax advantages but relinquish control over the assets once established. The tax benefits often outweigh the loss of control, particularly for high-net-worth individuals seeking to minimize estate and gift taxes. A well-structured irrevocable trust can protect assets from creditors and reduce your overall tax burden significantly, shielding your wealth from potential future liabilities.

Properly structuring your will and choosing the right type of trust requires a careful consideration of your personal circumstances and financial objectives. For example, if you anticipate significant estate taxes, an irrevocable trust might be beneficial, minimizing the tax liability for your heirs. For simpler estates with fewer assets, a will may suffice, especially when combined with beneficiary designations on retirement accounts and life insurance policies. However, even with straightforward estates, having a will provides peace of mind and ensures your wishes are carried out.

The choice between a will and a trust, or a combination of both, is not a one-size-fits-all solution. It's crucial to consult with an estate planning attorney to determine the best approach for your unique situation. An attorney can assist you in navigating the complexities of estate planning laws, ensuring your documents are legally sound and aligned with your goals. They can analyze your specific assets, family structure, and financial objectives, providing tailored advice and guidance. Remember, an estate planning attorney is not merely a legal advisor; they act as a strategic partner, helping you protect your legacy and secure the financial future of your loved ones.

Beyond the legal aspects, consider the emotional implications of estate planning. A well-crafted will and trust not only provide financial security but also

offer peace of mind, knowing your affairs are in order and your wishes will be respected. The process of creating these documents allows for reflection and ensures your family's future is protected, reducing potential conflicts and anxieties during a difficult time. This process should be viewed as a responsible step in managing your family's well-being, ensuring a smoother transition of assets and providing clarity for your loved ones. This proactive approach transforms estate planning from a daunting task into a comforting gesture of love and foresight.
Careful consideration should be given to the specific provisions within your will and trust. These documents should explicitly outline who will inherit your assets and under what conditions. Furthermore, clearly defining the roles and responsibilities of your executor and trustee is crucial for a smooth estate administration process. The executor is responsible for managing your estate, paying debts, and distributing assets according to your will, while the trustee manages assets within the trust according to its terms. Consider carefully the qualities needed for these roles – trustworthiness, financial acumen, and organizational skills are essential for effective management.
Finally, remember that estate planning is not a one-time event; it's an ongoing process. Your circumstances may change over time, requiring adjustments to your will and trust. Major life events like marriage, divorce, birth, or death necessitate a review of your estate plan to ensure it reflects your current wishes and circumstances. Regularly reviewing and updating your documents is crucial to maintain their effectiveness and avoid unintended consequences. Proactive estate planning offers peace of mind and safeguards your family's future. A carefully considered plan protects not only your assets but also your family's

emotional and financial well-being. By understanding the intricacies of wills and trusts and actively engaging in estate planning, you can secure a legacy that reflects your values and ensures the future prosperity of those you hold dear.

5.2 Gift & Estate Taxes

Understanding gift and estate taxes is crucial for high-net-worth individuals and families. These taxes, levied on the transfer of wealth during life (gifts) or at death (estate), can significantly impact your financial legacy. Effective planning minimizes these liabilities, ensuring a smoother transition of assets to your beneficiaries. Failing to plan adequately can result in substantial tax burdens, eating into the inheritance intended for your loved ones. Proactive planning provides a sense of security and control over the distribution of your assets.

The annual gift tax exclusion allows you to gift a certain amount of money each year to each recipient without incurring gift tax. This amount, adjusted annually for inflation, represents a significant advantage for estate planning. For example, by gifting assets each year, you gradually reduce the size of your taxable estate and, in turn, your potential estate tax liability. However, remember careful record-keeping is essential; you must accurately track all gifts to ensure compliance with IRS regulations. Overlooking this could lead to unintended tax consequences and potential penalties.

Gifting strategies often involve a combination of outright gifts and gifts to trusts. Outright gifts transfer ownership immediately, while gifts to trusts offer more control and flexibility. Trusts can provide asset protection, manage funds for beneficiaries, and potentially minimize tax liabilities. For instance, a grantor retained annuity trust (GRAT) allows you to transfer assets while potentially reducing the estate tax value. This is a more advanced strategy and consulting a tax professional is vital before implementing it. Careful consideration of your specific circumstances and long-term goals is crucial before choosing a particular approach.

Estate taxes, on the other hand, apply to the total value of your estate at death. The federal estate tax exemption is quite substantial; exceeding current limitations means you need to strategize. However, exceeding this amount triggers a tax. Many states also have their own estate taxes. This makes comprehensive estate planning, which incorporates both federal and state regulations, absolutely necessary. Understanding the nuances of both is crucial to effective tax minimization. This necessitates seeking professional advice, tailored to your unique circumstances and jurisdiction.

Strategies for minimizing estate taxes vary, but often incorporate a combination of techniques. These could include charitable giving, which deducts the value of donations from your estate; life insurance policies structured to minimize tax implications; and carefully planned asset distributions before death. Such strategies, however, require meticulous planning and are often complex to implement. Consult a qualified estate planner and tax attorney to ensure legal compliance. They can assist you in exploring and implementing sophisticated techniques effectively, mitigating risks, and guaranteeing a smooth and efficient asset transfer.

Consider the impact of probate, the legal process of distributing assets after death. Probate can be time-consuming and expensive, especially for large or complex estates. Careful planning can often minimize or even eliminate the need for probate through strategies like the use of trusts. Trusts allow for the management and distribution of assets outside of probate court, providing efficiency, privacy, and cost-effectiveness for your beneficiaries. It simplifies the transfer of assets, and protects your family from lengthy legal processes.

It's essential to regularly review your estate plan, as tax laws and your personal circumstances can change significantly. What worked effectively five years ago may not be the optimal strategy today. Regularly scheduled reviews with your financial team help ensure your estate plan remains current and aligned with your goals. This ongoing maintenance and adaptation prevent unforeseen issues later and makes sure everything is updated according to changes in laws and life events. Ignoring these reviews can have devastating financial and legal consequences.

Finally, remember that this chapter is for informational purposes only and does not constitute legal or financial advice. Due to the complexity of gift and estate taxes, it is vital to consult with qualified professionals—including a tax attorney and a financial advisor—to develop a personalized plan that addresses your specific situation and meets your long-term goals. Their expertise ensures your estate plan is both effective and compliant with all applicable laws and regulations. This professional guidance is indispensable for mitigating risk and securing the financial well-being of your beneficiaries.

5.3 Beneficiary Designations

Beneficiary designations are crucial for estate planning, allowing you to direct the distribution of your assets after your death. Properly utilizing these designations can significantly minimize estate taxes and ensure your loved ones receive their inheritance efficiently and effectively. Ignoring this step often leads to unintended consequences, potentially causing delays, disputes, and unnecessary tax burdens for your heirs. Think of it as a roadmap, guiding your assets to their intended destinations.

Understanding the various types of beneficiary designations is paramount. You'll encounter several options depending on the asset: retirement accounts, life insurance policies, bank accounts, and investment accounts all have their own specific designation processes. For example, with a retirement account like a 401(k) or IRA, you can name a primary beneficiary and a contingent beneficiary. This provides a clear succession plan, ensuring the assets are transferred smoothly if your primary beneficiary predeceases you. Similarly, life insurance policies often use the same system, protecting your beneficiaries from potential complications. However, it's vital to regularly review and update these designations to reflect changes in your family structure or financial goals. A simple oversight here can have severe ramifications.

The choice of beneficiary significantly impacts tax liability. For instance, designating a spouse as a beneficiary often results in favorable tax treatment, while naming other individuals might trigger tax consequences. Depending on the relationship and the specific asset, the inheritance might be subject to estate taxes, income taxes, or both. Understanding these tax implications is crucial. It's advisable to consult with a qualified financial advisor or tax professional to carefully analyze your unique situation and determine the most tax-efficient approach for your specific circumstances. They can provide invaluable guidance, ensuring you make informed decisions that align with your long-term financial objectives. Don't underestimate the importance of professional advice in this area; it can save your family considerable money and heartache.

Moreover, you should consider the legal implications of your beneficiary designations. State laws and specific provisions in your estate plan play a significant role in the distribution process. For example, some states have specific rules regarding community property, potentially impacting how assets are divided between spouses. Likewise, any existing trusts or other estate planning documents will interact with your beneficiary designations, potentially altering the distribution of assets. It's imperative to ensure that your beneficiary designations are consistent with the overall goals of your estate plan and comply with all relevant laws. A misalignment here can lead to protracted legal battles, significantly impacting your loved ones' ability to access their inheritance promptly and efficiently.

Furthermore, your beneficiary designations need regular updates. Life is unpredictable, and your circumstances inevitably change. Marriage, divorce, the birth of children, or even a significant shift in your financial priorities necessitate revisiting your beneficiary designations. Failing to update them can lead to assets going to unintended recipients, causing considerable distress and financial complications. For instance, if you divorce but neglect to update your beneficiary designation on a retirement account, your ex-spouse might still inherit a significant portion of those assets upon your passing. This scenario highlights the critical importance of reviewing and adjusting your beneficiary designations at various milestones in your life, ensuring the designations remain current and accurate. A well-maintained plan offers peace of mind, knowing your assets will be distributed according to your wishes.

Finally, the process of updating beneficiary designations is often simpler than you might imagine. Most institutions provide straightforward forms and instructions on their websites or in their offices. For retirement accounts, you usually just need to complete a simple form and submit it to the plan administrator. For life insurance policies, you may need to update the information with your insurance provider. It's a small task with significant long-term implications, one that offers substantial protection against potential problems. Don't procrastinate; take action today. The peace of mind that comes with knowing your assets are safely directed to your chosen beneficiaries is invaluable. Remember, a small effort now can prevent significant complications and potential disputes for your family in the future.

6 Chapter 6: Tax-Efficient Businesses

Selecting the right business structure is crucial for minimizing your tax burden. A sole proprietorship, the simplest form, blends your personal and business finances, meaning all profits are taxed as personal income. However, this also allows for easy deduction of business expenses directly against your personal income, potentially leading to lower overall taxes if your expenses are high. This simplicity can be attractive to those just starting, though it offers less liability protection.

Conversely, an S corporation offers a degree of separation. Profits are passed through to the owner's personal income tax return, but you can pay yourself a salary and take the remaining profits as distributions, potentially reducing your self-employment tax liability. This structure requires more paperwork, including meticulous record-keeping, and may involve higher accounting fees. Careful planning and accurate record-keeping are essential here to avoid penalties. Understanding the nuances of this structure is paramount for optimal tax efficiency, demanding a higher level of financial literacy or professional guidance.

Limited Liability Companies (LLCs) provide flexibility. They can be taxed as sole proprietorships, partnerships, or S corporations, offering adaptable tax treatment based on your specific circumstances and financial objectives. This flexibility allows you to choose the structure that best aligns with your current income level and long-term financial plans, optimizing for tax efficiency at each stage of your business's growth. However, this flexibility comes with the added complexity of needing to thoroughly understand the implications of each tax option and accurately determining the most beneficial choice.

Partnerships, involving two or more individuals, offer shared responsibility and diverse expertise but necessitate a thorough understanding of partnership agreements and tax implications. Profit and loss are shared among partners and reported on individual tax returns, impacting each partner's overall tax liability. Clearly defined roles, responsibilities, and profit-sharing arrangements within the partnership agreement are crucial to prevent future disputes and to ensure accurate tax reporting. The complexities inherent in partnerships underscore the need for competent legal and financial counsel.

Choosing the right structure requires careful consideration of several factors. Your projected income, the level of risk you're willing to accept, the complexity of your business operations, and your long-term goals all play a significant role. Consulting with a tax professional is highly recommended; they can assess your specific circumstances and advise on the structure that best suits your needs, ensuring you optimize your tax strategy from the outset. This proactive approach minimizes future complications and ensures compliance with all relevant tax regulations. Ignoring professional advice can lead to considerable financial setbacks.

Beyond the fundamental structure, several business tax credits can further reduce your tax burden. These credits, offered at various levels of government, often incentivize specific business activities or investment. Researching and identifying relevant credits is crucial. Credits, unlike deductions, directly reduce your tax liability, offering a more substantial impact on your overall tax bill. Familiarizing yourself with available credits can significantly improve your tax efficiency. However, qualifying for these credits requires compliance with specific eligibility requirements, which necessitates detailed understanding of the terms and conditions. Consulting a tax professional to identify and leverage applicable credits is highly advisable to avoid potential errors and missed opportunities. Taking advantage of these credits can significantly boost the profitability of your venture, allowing for reinvestment and further expansion. Regularly review available credits, as they can change based on legislation, economic conditions and your company's performance. Understanding tax credits requires sustained effort and attention to detail.

Effective tax planning isn't a one-time event; it's an ongoing process. Regularly reviewing your business structure and exploring available tax credits ensures you remain compliant and maximize your after-tax profits. This commitment to ongoing optimization is a fundamental aspect of building a successful, financially sound business. The long-term benefits of careful, proactive tax planning far outweigh the initial effort involved. Remember, a well-structured, tax-efficient business is a foundation for long-term financial security and sustainable growth. The proactive management of your tax obligations protects your earnings and lays the groundwork for the achievement of your overall business and financial goals.

6.1 Sole Proprietorship

A sole proprietorship, the simplest business structure, blends your personal and business finances. This means you, the owner, are directly responsible for all business profits and losses, and these flow directly onto your personal tax return, Schedule C. While this simplicity offers ease of setup, requiring minimal paperwork beyond registering your business name (in many jurisdictions, this isn't even legally required), it also comes with significant tax implications that require careful consideration. Understanding these nuances is crucial to minimize your overall tax burden.

One major advantage is the simplicity of filing. You report all business income and expenses on your individual tax return, streamlining the process considerably compared to more complex structures like corporations. This minimizes the need for separate accounting practices, reducing both your time investment and the fees you might pay to a professional accountant. This direct reporting makes it easier to track your income and expenses throughout the year, improving your financial management skills and providing a clearer picture of your business's overall performance. The resulting clarity allows for quicker and more efficient tax preparation.

However, this simplicity also creates unlimited liability. This means your personal assets – your house, car, savings – are at risk should your business incur debt or face lawsuits. Unlike corporations or LLCs which offer some level of legal protection, a sole proprietorship puts everything on the line. Therefore, robust personal liability insurance is not just advisable, it's essential to safeguard your personal finances. This extra cost, however, is offset, at least in part, by the simpler administrative burden. Weighing these pros and cons is a crucial first step in determining the best fit for your business.

Tax planning becomes exceptionally important within a sole proprietorship. Because your business income is directly taxed as personal income, strategically managing deductions becomes paramount. Meticulously track all business-related expenses, from office supplies and utilities to travel costs and professional development courses. Maintain detailed records; this diligent record-keeping protects you from potential audits and helps you fully utilize every allowable deduction. Remember, accurate record-keeping is not just about minimizing taxes; it's about gaining a holistic understanding of your business finances, facilitating better decision-making and providing a clearer financial picture.

While the IRS allows you to deduct many business expenses, remember that some costs are disallowed entirely, while others are partially deductible, with specific limitations and restrictions applied. This is especially relevant when claiming home office deductions, a common expense for sole proprietors working from home. Thorough research and, if necessary, professional tax advice, are vital to understanding the exact rules and regulations for claiming these crucial deductions, and to ensure compliance with all relevant legislation and regulations. It might seem intimidating, yet a clear grasp of these regulations provides a distinct advantage in minimizing your tax obligations.

Consider also the potential impact of self-employment taxes. As a sole proprietor, you're responsible for paying both the employer and employee portions of Social Security and Medicare taxes. This contrasts with traditional employment where your employer typically covers half. While this doubles your tax burden in this respect, strategic tax planning can help mitigate this, and many tax-advantaged plans help buffer this significant cost. Understanding these self-employment taxes is essential for budgeting and accurate financial forecasting, helping you make informed decisions about your business and personal finances.

Retirement planning within a sole proprietorship requires proactive measures. Unlike traditional employees with employer-sponsored plans, you are responsible for establishing and contributing to your own retirement fund. Options include SEP IRAs or solo 401(k)s, both offering tax advantages to help you save for retirement. Understanding the contribution limits, eligibility requirements, and potential tax benefits associated with each is crucial for effective retirement planning. These plans offer unique and often significant tax benefits, and exploring them thoroughly ensures a secure and comfortable financial future.

In conclusion, the sole proprietorship offers simplicity in setup and administration, but it requires meticulous attention to detail regarding tax compliance and liability. While the ease of filing is a significant advantage, the unlimited personal liability necessitates robust insurance. Proactive tax planning, including meticulous record-keeping and understanding allowable deductions, is not merely advisable; it's essential for minimizing your tax burden and protecting your personal assets. Furthermore, responsible retirement planning is crucial to ensure a financially secure future. The seemingly simple structure of a sole proprietorship requires informed financial management for long-term success.

6.2 S Corporations & LLCs

S corporations and limited liability companies (LLCs) offer distinct advantages for tax optimization, but their suitability depends heavily on individual circumstances. Understanding the core differences is crucial for making an informed decision that aligns with your financial goals. A key difference lies in the way profits and losses are handled. S corporations, for example, distribute profits and losses to shareholders based on their ownership stake, reflecting their individual tax brackets, potentially resulting in lower overall tax liability compared to a sole proprietorship where business income is taxed as personal income. Conversely, LLCs typically don't have this pass-through feature, though they allow flexibility in how profits and losses are allocated. This means careful consideration of the member's personal tax situation is crucial for maximizing efficiency.

Choosing between an S corp and an LLC involves navigating a complex landscape of legal and tax implications. The administrative burden of an S corp is often greater than an LLC, requiring more stringent compliance procedures and record-keeping. Annual meetings, for example, are mandated for S corporations, increasing administrative tasks. LLCs tend to offer more flexibility and fewer formal requirements, making them attractive to those seeking streamlined administrative processes. This administrative ease may be particularly beneficial for newer business ventures, allowing them to concentrate on growth rather than complex compliance issues. For larger businesses with significant revenue streams, however, the added complexity of an S corp might be worth the potential tax advantages.

Beyond the initial setup, ongoing compliance differs significantly. The Internal Revenue Service (IRS) imposes stricter reporting requirements on S corporations than on LLCs, demanding more detailed financial documentation. This includes stricter adherence to corporate formalities, such as holding regular meetings and maintaining meticulous records of shareholder transactions. Failure to comply with these rigorous requirements can result in penalties and loss of the favorable S corp tax status. For smaller operations, the added paperwork involved might represent a significant increase in administrative costs, possibly negating the overall tax benefits. LLCs offer greater simplicity, minimizing the compliance burden and making them an easier option for many entrepreneurs. Tax implications extend beyond the simple pass-through of income and losses. The IRS treats S corporations and LLCs differently regarding certain deductions, impacting the overall tax savings. For instance, S corporations are allowed to deduct a reasonable salary paid to their shareholders; a strategic move that can reduce taxable income. On the other hand, LLCs may not have the same flexibility in deducting owner compensation. Moreover, benefits provided to employees, such as health insurance, often receive favorable tax treatment for S corporations, though the specific rules can be complex and require professional tax advice. The nuances of these deductions must be carefully considered and understood.

The optimal choice between an S corporation and an LLC depends on a nuanced analysis of various factors. For example, projected income levels significantly influence the decision. High-income individuals might benefit more from the potential tax advantages of an S corporation, despite the increased administrative complexities. Conversely, entrepreneurs with lower projected income could find the simpler setup of an LLC more advantageous. The number of owners is another deciding factor, as the relative administrative burdens might outweigh the benefits of choosing one over another. Consulting with a tax professional is always advisable to determine the most beneficial structure. This professional guidance ensures an accurate assessment of your individual circumstances and a tailored strategy.

Ultimately, the choice boils down to balancing tax advantages against administrative burden. Both S corporations and LLCs offer unique opportunities for tax optimization, but the ideal structure varies based on your specific needs, the predicted financial performance of the business, and your tolerance for administrative complexities. It's important to consider your long-term goals and projected growth before committing to a particular business structure. Engaging an accountant or tax attorney will help analyze your individual circumstances and will assist you in making the best possible decision, which ultimately protects your future financial success and helps you remain in compliance with applicable legal regulations. Remember, minimizing tax burden involves far more than just choosing the right structure; it also involves diligent record-keeping and adherence to tax laws, which ultimately contribute to your long-term financial well-being.

6.3 Partnerships

Partnerships offer a compelling blend of liability protection and tax advantages, making them an attractive option for many businesses. Unlike sole proprietorships, where personal and business liabilities are intertwined, a partnership shields personal assets from business debts. This separation is a crucial element, providing a safety net against potential financial setbacks. However, this protection isn't absolute; the level of protection depends largely on the specific type of partnership established and the state's laws governing it. Understanding these intricacies is essential for minimizing risks.

The tax implications of a partnership are significantly different from those of a sole proprietorship or even an LLC. In a partnership, profits and losses are "passed through" to the individual partners, meaning they are reported on the partners' personal income tax returns, rather than the partnership itself filing a separate tax return. This pass-through structure avoids double taxation, a significant benefit compared to corporations. This is a key advantage, allowing partners to potentially reduce their overall tax burden. Yet, it requires meticulous record-keeping and careful tax planning to ensure compliance and optimize tax benefits. Each partner reports their share of the partnership's income or losses on their individual return. The allocation of income and losses must be clearly defined in the partnership agreement to avoid disputes and ensure accurate reporting. This requires careful consideration and potentially, the advice of a tax professional.

Choosing the right type of partnership is crucial. A general partnership offers simplicity but exposes all partners to unlimited liability. Conversely, a limited partnership (LP) provides some partners with limited liability, making it a more suitable structure for ventures with higher risk. Limited liability partnerships (LLPs) offer similar protection. Understanding the nuances of each type and selecting the one aligning with your specific business needs and risk tolerance is key. An ill-considered choice can have significant repercussions, both financially and legally. A consultation with a legal and financial professional will ensure that you select the correct structure for your business and its financial goals. This crucial step should not be overlooked.

Beyond the fundamental structure, strategic tax planning within a partnership is vital. Effective tax planning involves proactively identifying and utilizing deductions to minimize taxable income. Deductible expenses may include business-related travel, supplies, and professional fees. Meticulous record-keeping is paramount for substantiating these deductions. Proper documentation provides protection against potential audits and ensures a smooth tax filing process. A well-organized filing system is a small price to pay for the peace of mind it offers. This careful approach will prevent problems later on.

Furthermore, optimizing the distribution of profits among partners can also impact the overall tax liability. Careful consideration of each partner's individual tax bracket and situation can lead to significant savings. This strategy requires a deep understanding of the tax code and the financial profiles of all partners involved in the business. In many cases, engaging a tax advisor to model different distribution scenarios can reveal significant tax optimization opportunities. Their expertise can help avoid unintentional tax implications. Remember, maximizing tax efficiency is not just about minimizing taxes, but also about long-term financial planning and wealth accumulation.

Beyond the immediate tax benefits, establishing a strong partnership agreement is critical for long-term success. This legal document should clearly define the responsibilities, profit-sharing arrangements, dispute resolution mechanisms, and the process for adding or removing partners. A well-drafted agreement protects all parties involved, preventing future conflicts and ensuring a smooth operational flow. This foresight contributes significantly to overall stability and minimizes potential legal issues. Neglecting this step might lead to disputes, potentially derailing the business.

The intricacies of partnerships—from legal structuring to ongoing tax planning—underscore the importance of professional guidance. Engaging tax advisors, legal counsel, and potentially financial planners can prove invaluable. These professionals bring expertise and experience, helping navigate the complexities of the tax code and ensuring that your partnership is structured and operated in a way that maximizes benefits while minimizing potential risks. This professional guidance ensures that every decision made supports long-term success. Their knowledge will help you avoid costly mistakes.

Finally, remember that the partnership structure is not a one-size-fits-all solution. Thoroughly evaluate your specific circumstances, considering your business goals, risk tolerance, and the financial profiles of all involved partners. This careful evaluation is paramount. Only after this assessment should you make a decision. The choice of a partnership should be a deliberate and informed one, guided by sound legal and financial advice. Don't rush into this decision. A hasty decision might lead to regrettable consequences. Take the time you need.

6.4 Choosing the Right Structure

Choosing the right business structure is crucial for long-term financial success. The structure you select directly impacts your tax liability, liability protection, and administrative burden. Ignoring this decision can lead to significant financial penalties down the line, severely impacting your bottom line. Careful consideration of your specific needs is paramount.

A sole proprietorship, the simplest structure, blends your personal and business finances. This means all business income is reported on your personal tax return, simplifying accounting but offering minimal liability protection. Your personal assets are at risk should your business face legal issues. This lack of separation is a considerable drawback, especially for businesses with significant risk or liability exposure. Consider this option only if your business is truly small and low-risk.

Alternatively, a partnership combines the resources and expertise of two or more individuals. While offering some benefits of shared responsibility and increased capital, it also carries shared liability. Each partner is personally responsible for the debts and liabilities of the business. This can be advantageous in some instances but represents a significant risk if one partner faces financial difficulties. Thoroughly vetting partners and clearly defining responsibilities within a well-structured partnership agreement is essential.

Limited Liability Companies (LLCs) offer a significant advantage: liability protection. An LLC separates your personal assets from business liabilities, shielding your personal wealth from business debts or lawsuits. This is a crucial factor for businesses with higher risk profiles. The taxation of an LLC can be flexible;

it can be taxed as a sole proprietorship, partnership, or corporation, providing adaptable tax optimization depending on your specific circumstances and projected income. This flexibility is a compelling advantage.

S corporations, a more complex structure, offer pass-through taxation, meaning profits and losses are passed through to the owners' personal tax returns, avoiding double taxation common in traditional corporations. However, stringent requirements must be met to qualify for S corporation status. These requirements include limitations on the number of shareholders and restrictions on the types of stock issued. This structure is generally suitable for businesses with a more established history and significant income levels, needing more sophisticated tax planning strategies.

The selection process involves weighing these factors against your individual circumstances. Consider the size and complexity of your business, your risk tolerance, and your long-term financial goals. The tax implications of each structure vary widely based on factors such as your income level, deductions, and credits available. It is advisable to consult with a qualified tax professional who can provide personalized guidance based on your specific business and financial situation.

Remember that the choice isn't permanent. As your business grows and evolves, your chosen structure might need to adapt to maintain optimal tax efficiency and liability protection. Regular review of your business structure is prudent. Failing to do so could inadvertently expose you to unnecessary financial risks. Proactive planning is essential for minimizing your tax burdens and maximizing your long-term prosperity. Seeking professional advice early will pay dividends in the long run, safeguarding both your financial well-being and the future of your enterprise. Don't underestimate the significance of this crucial decision. Your business's success hinges significantly on making an informed and strategic choice.

6.5 Business Tax Credits

Understanding business tax credits can significantly reduce your tax burden. These credits, unlike deductions, directly reduce the amount of tax you owe, offering a more impactful benefit than simply lowering your taxable income. Many credits are available, each with specific eligibility requirements and limitations. Careful research is crucial to determine which credits apply to your specific business and situation. Remember, consulting with a tax professional is always recommended to ensure you're maximizing your benefits legally and efficiently. Don't overlook this potent tool for minimizing your tax liability; it could be a substantial financial advantage.

The Research and Development (R&D) tax credit is a prime example of a valuable business tax credit. It rewards companies for investing in innovation, offering a significant incentive for research and development activities. Eligibility criteria vary based on the type of research conducted and the specific industry. Qualifying expenses include salaries, supplies, and contract research costs, among others. The credit is calculated based on qualified expenses, and the percentage of the credit can fluctuate depending on the type of research and the company's size. Proper documentation is paramount for claiming this credit, so meticulous record-keeping is essential throughout the research process. This credit can significantly impact a company's bottom line, boosting financial health and future innovation.

For small businesses, the Work Opportunity Tax Credit (WOTC) presents a compelling opportunity for tax savings. This credit incentivizes hiring individuals from specific disadvantaged groups, including veterans, ex-offenders, and those from long-term unemployment. The credit amount varies depending on the employee's characteristics and the number of hours worked. To claim the WOTC, employers must obtain a pre-hire certification from the Department of Labor. This certification verifies the employee's eligibility, ensuring the credit can be claimed accurately. The administrative hurdles involved may seem daunting, but the financial reward for supporting these communities significantly outweighs the effort, creating an ethical and financially smart decision.

The general business credit is a catch-all category encompassing several different credits. This umbrella credit includes the R&D credit, WOTC, and many others discussed earlier, combining them into a singular tax advantage. The calculation of the general business credit can be complex and often involves multiple components. It's usually limited to a certain percentage of your income tax liability, further highlighting the importance of precise and accurate record keeping. Understanding the intricacies of the general business credit requires a solid grasp of all its individual components, making a consultation with a tax advisor an invaluable asset.

Energy-efficient improvements can also yield significant tax benefits. The Energy Efficient Commercial Building Deduction provides incentives for businesses investing in energy-efficient upgrades, promoting sustainability and lowering operational costs. Improvements include upgrades to heating, ventilation, and air conditioning (HVAC) systems, insulation, and other energy-saving technologies. The deduction amount depends on the type and cost of the improvements, making it imperative to carefully track all expenses related to the project. This deduction not only helps your environment, but it also provides significant tax relief, demonstrating a positive impact on both profits and the planet. Beyond the previously mentioned credits, numerous others exist, each tailored to specific industries or business activities. These can range from credits for hiring apprentices to credits for investing in renewable energy technologies or expanding businesses into certain underserved areas. The availability and eligibility requirements for these credits fluctuate, requiring consistent monitoring of legislative changes and regulations. Staying informed about these developments is critical for maximizing the tax advantages your business can enjoy. Proactive research combined with expert guidance is paramount to securing these financial opportunities.

Many resources are available to assist in navigating the complexities of business tax credits. The Internal Revenue Service (IRS) website provides detailed information on all available credits, along with eligibility guidelines and instructions for claiming them. Numerous tax software programs and online resources also offer valuable tools and guidance, streamlining the process of identifying and claiming applicable credits. Remember, while these resources are helpful, consulting with a qualified tax professional remains crucial for accurate claim preparation and optimal tax optimization. Their expertise ensures compliance and identifies credits often overlooked.

The success of effectively utilizing business tax credits hinges on meticulous record-keeping. Maintaining detailed records of all qualifying expenses and activities is essential for substantiating your claim. These records should be easily accessible and organized for audit purposes. A well-organized filing system, coupled with accurate documentation, will significantly increase the chances of a successful tax credit claim, potentially saving you a considerable sum of money. Take the time to maintain these files; your fiscal future depends on this detail. It could make the difference between a considerable tax refund and a significant penalty.

Finally, remember that the tax code is subject to change. Legislation affecting business tax credits evolves regularly; therefore, staying informed about these changes is crucial for maximizing your tax advantages. Following developments in tax law through reputable sources such as government websites and professional journals is advisable. Consider this ongoing education part of your business management; this active engagement with updated legislation significantly improves your business' financial standing. This continued learning keeps your strategy current and efficient.

7 Chapter 7: Advanced Tax Strategies

Tax loss harvesting offers a powerful, yet often overlooked, opportunity to significantly reduce your tax burden. Imagine this: you've had some successful investments, generating capital gains. Simultaneously, you've experienced losses in other areas. Instead of simply accepting those losses, tax loss harvesting allows you to strategically sell your losing assets, offsetting your capital gains and lowering your overall taxable income. This isn't about avoiding paying taxes; it's about legally minimizing your tax liability using existing regulations. This technique requires careful planning and an understanding of your investment portfolio's performance. Timing is crucial; you need to sell the losing assets before the end of the tax year to realize the loss. Consulting a qualified financial advisor can prove invaluable in optimizing this strategy for your specific circumstances. Remember, the goal isn't to incur losses; it's to strategically manage existing ones to your advantage.

Understanding the intricacies of various tax credits and incentives can unlock substantial savings. Unlike deductions, which reduce your taxable income, credits directly reduce the amount of tax you owe, dollar for dollar. The availability of these credits often depends on your income, filing status, and specific life circumstances. For example, the Child Tax Credit can provide significant relief for families with qualifying children. Other credits might be available for education expenses, home energy improvements, or even for purchasing a new electric vehicle. Many specialized credits exist for specific industries or situations, so thorough research is vital. Don't assume you're ineligible for any credits; exploring the possibilities is always worthwhile. The IRS website and professional tax advice can be your best resources for identifying and claiming the credits you are entitled to.

Beyond the commonly known credits, consider exploring less-familiar options. The Earned Income Tax Credit (EITC), for instance, helps low-to-moderate-income working individuals and families. Depending on your income and family size, this credit could provide a significant refund. Other, potentially less advertised incentives, such as those related to renewable energy investments or certain types of business expenditures, can also dramatically lower your taxes. These incentives often have specific requirements, deadlines, and forms. Meticulous record-keeping is paramount, as you'll need detailed documentation to claim these credits. Proactive research and preparation are essential for maximizing the benefits of less-prominent tax credits and incentives.

Strategically combining tax loss harvesting with the utilization of tax credits can be incredibly effective. Imagine a scenario where you've had capital gains, but you also qualify for the Child Tax Credit. By strategically harvesting losses to offset some gains, you reduce your taxable income and then directly reduce your tax owed by claiming the available credit. This combination approach exemplifies the synergistic potential of leveraging multiple tax-saving strategies. The outcome is a more significant reduction in your overall tax liability than using each strategy in isolation. However, it's crucial to remember that timing is everything. Careful coordination is required to ensure the optimal utilization of both methods within the constraints of tax deadlines.

Advanced tax planning extends beyond simple deductions and credits. It involves a proactive and holistic approach to your financial life. It's not simply about minimizing your current tax bill, but about strategically structuring your finances to maximize long-term benefits. This requires a thorough understanding of your income, expenses, investments, and future financial goals. A comprehensive financial plan should integrate tax considerations into all aspects of your financial strategy, such as retirement planning, estate planning, and business structuring, creating a cohesive framework for tax optimization. This requires constant review and adjustment as your circumstances evolve.

A key aspect of advanced tax planning is proactive engagement with tax professionals. While many individuals manage their taxes independently using software or basic guides, seeking advice from experienced tax advisors can prove invaluable. These professionals possess in-depth knowledge of current tax laws, regulations, and available strategies. They can help you identify opportunities you might have overlooked and navigate the complexities of tax codes. They can provide personalized guidance tailored to your specific financial situation and assist with preparing and filing your tax returns accurately and efficiently. Don't hesitate to utilize their expertise to minimize your risks and maximize your tax benefits. A small investment in professional advice can often yield substantial long-term savings.

Finally, remember that tax laws are constantly evolving. Staying informed about changes and updates is crucial for maintaining tax compliance and taking advantage of new opportunities. Regularly review your tax strategy and adjust it as needed to align with the latest regulations. Subscribing to relevant publications, attending tax seminars, and maintaining ongoing communication with your tax advisor are all excellent ways to stay abreast of developments and ensure your tax planning remains effective and legally sound. Proactive tax management isn't a one-time endeavor; it's an ongoing process that requires vigilance and adaptation. By consistently reviewing your strategies and staying informed about changes, you'll maintain control over your tax obligations and secure a more robust financial future.

7.1 Tax Loss Harvesting

Tax loss harvesting is a powerful strategy to reduce your tax burden. It involves selling investments that have lost value to offset capital gains from investments that have appreciated. This isn't about avoiding taxes altogether; it's about legally minimizing your tax liability, something perfectly permissible and encouraged within the framework of sound financial planning. Think of it as a smart way to play the system to your advantage.

The core principle is straightforward: losses offset gains. If you have a capital gain of $10,000, you can offset that with $10,000 in capital losses, resulting in no taxable capital gains in that year. Importantly, you can only deduct up to $3,000 ($1,500 if married filing separately) in losses annually against your ordinary income. However, any excess loss can be carried forward to reduce your tax liability in future years. This carry-forward provision is incredibly useful for long-term tax planning, allowing you to strategically manage your capital gains over multiple years.

Remember, this isn't a get-rich-quick scheme; it's a long-term strategy requiring careful planning and consideration. It's crucial to consult with a qualified financial advisor. They can help you determine which investments to sell, considering factors like your overall investment portfolio, risk tolerance, and financial goals. Don't make impulsive decisions based solely on short-term market fluctuations. A good advisor will help you craft a comprehensive plan tailored to your specific situation. They will consider factors that extend beyond simply identifying losses, factors such as future investment strategies, overall tax liability, and your risk appetite.

For example, imagine you're a seasoned investor with a diversified portfolio. You've noticed some losses in specific stock positions, and you're about to sell profitable assets to fund a new venture. A tax loss harvest strategy could significantly reduce the tax bite from those profitable sales. By strategically selling the losing assets first, you can use those losses to offset the gains, potentially saving thousands of dollars in taxes. This saved money could then be reinvested, further fueling your new venture's growth. This exemplifies the power of intelligent tax planning to enhance your financial success.

The process of tax loss harvesting isn't overly complicated. You'll need to identify your capital losses, carefully evaluate which assets to sell, and then execute the trades appropriately. The timing is critical. It is often best to sell losing assets before the end of the tax year to take advantage of the current year's deduction. Postponing it can reduce your immediate tax liability but might limit your ability to carry forward losses if you exceed the annual limitation. Remember to keep detailed records of all your transactions, including the purchase date and price, the sale date and price, and any applicable fees. This meticulous record-keeping is crucial for accurate tax reporting.

However, there's a crucial caveat to be aware of – the wash-sale rule. This rule prevents you from claiming a loss if you repurchase substantially identical securities within 30 days before or after the sale. This means that while you're realizing a loss and thus reducing your taxes, you can't immediately reinvest in the same asset to try and recover the loss. For example, if you sold shares of XYZ stock at a loss and then bought similar shares of XYZ within 30 days, the loss is disallowed, and the cost basis of the new shares will include the loss to reflect your ultimate cost. Your tax advisor can guide you through navigating these complexities.

The benefits extend beyond immediate tax savings. Tax loss harvesting can improve your overall portfolio's tax efficiency in the long run. By strategically managing your capital gains and losses, you can minimize your overall tax burden over time, thereby maximizing your investment returns. It allows you to maintain a balanced portfolio while optimizing your tax situation, a delicate balancing act best accomplished with professional guidance. This strategic approach is a critical component of long-term financial health and growth.

Moreover, understanding tax loss harvesting helps you to make more informed investment decisions. It encourages a more disciplined approach to investing, prompting you to evaluate the tax implications of your trades rather than solely focusing on immediate market gains. Instead of simply chasing returns, it shifts your perspective to view investing through the lens of tax efficiency, allowing for a potentially greater return overall.

In conclusion, tax loss harvesting is not a magical solution to eliminate taxes completely. However, when implemented thoughtfully and strategically, it can significantly reduce your tax liability and enhance your investment returns. This is a sophisticated strategy that requires careful consideration and professional advice. By incorporating this technique into your overall investment and tax planning strategy, you can improve your financial well-being. Remember to consult with a qualified financial advisor to ensure it aligns with your specific financial situation and long-term goals. The careful execution of this strategy can make a notable difference to your financial future.

7.2 Tax Credits & Incentives

Tax credits and incentives offer a powerful, often overlooked, avenue for significant tax savings. Unlike deductions, which reduce your taxable income, credits directly reduce your tax liability, dollar for dollar. Understanding and utilizing these credits can be the difference between a substantial tax bill and a significantly smaller one, freeing up funds for investments, savings, or other personal goals. Many such opportunities exist, tailored to specific circumstances and require proactive research.

Finding the right credits requires a thorough understanding of your individual financial situation. Are you a homeowner? Do you have children? Are you investing in renewable energy? These seemingly simple questions can unlock a plethora of potential credits. For example, the Residential Energy Efficient Property Credit rewards homeowners for making energy-efficient improvements, such as installing solar panels or energy-efficient windows. The Child Tax Credit provides substantial relief for families with qualifying children, directly reducing their tax burden.

The Earned Income Tax Credit (EITC) is particularly beneficial for low-to-moderate-income working individuals and families. It's a refundable credit, meaning you can receive a refund even if the credit exceeds your tax liability. This makes it a powerful tool for those who often struggle with financial stability. Eligibility criteria, however, are very specific, based on income, filing status, and the number of qualifying children. To maximize your benefit, carefully review the IRS guidelines, as changes are occasionally implemented.

Beyond personal circumstances, consider business-related credits. If you own a small business, numerous credits could significantly impact your bottom line. The Work Opportunity Tax Credit, for instance, incentivizes hiring individuals from certain disadvantaged groups. The research and experimentation credit can offset expenses incurred for qualifying research activities, fostering innovation and development. Careful planning and accurate record-keeping are crucial to maximize these opportunities. Incorrectly completed forms can easily nullify your eligibility for the benefits you might otherwise reap.

Navigating the complexities of tax credits and incentives can feel overwhelming. The sheer number of available credits, along with the specific requirements for each, necessitates a strategic approach. Beginning with a thorough review of the IRS publications relevant to your situation is essential. Consider consulting with a tax professional—a certified public accountant (CPA) or enrolled agent—to ensure you're taking full advantage of all applicable credits. Their expertise ensures you're complying with all regulations, maximizing your credits, and avoiding costly mistakes.

Remember, proactively researching and planning for tax credits and incentives is crucial. Don't wait until the last minute. Thoroughly review your financial situation throughout the year, identifying potential credit opportunities as they arise. Keep accurate records of all qualifying expenses, and gather all necessary documentation well in advance of tax season. This proactive approach will maximize your return and minimize the stress associated with tax preparation.

Furthermore, the landscape of tax credits and incentives is dynamic. Regulations and eligibility requirements can change annually. Staying informed about updates and changes to the tax code is critical to maintaining compliance and accessing the latest beneficial opportunities. Regularly reviewing IRS publications and tax newsletters is highly advisable, providing updates in an easily digestible form. Subscription to trusted sources on taxation matters can increase your access to updated information.

Finally, the benefits extend beyond just immediate tax savings. The strategic utilization of tax credits and incentives can positively shape your long-term financial health. By reducing your tax liability, you free up resources for investments, retirement savings, or paying down debt. This, in turn, leads to greater financial security and peace of mind. Effective tax planning is not simply about minimizing taxes; it's about achieving your overall financial goals effectively. Consider this as a crucial element of a holistic financial strategy.

Don't underestimate the power of tax credits and incentives. They represent a significant opportunity to reduce your tax burden and build a stronger financial future. The effort invested in understanding and utilizing them yields a substantial return. A small amount of proactive effort during the year can significantly reduce your tax liability. Remember, claiming your credits isn't just about compliance; it's about taking control of your financial well-being. So, start exploring the options today; it could be more beneficial than you initially thought.

www.ingramcontent.com/pod-product-compliance
Lightning Source LLC
LaVergne TN
LVHW022016200926
848481LV00007B/2419